鲁拜集

[波斯]欧马尔·海亚姆 著
[英]爱德华·菲兹杰德拉 英译 | 曾记（译）

中山大學出版社
·广州·

版权所有　翻印必究

图书在版编目（CIP）数据

鲁拜集／[波斯]欧玛尔·海亚姆（Omar Khayyam）著；[英]爱德华·菲兹杰拉德（Edward FitzGerald）英译；曾记译. —广州：中山大学出版社，2017.10
　ISBN 978-7-306-06196-6

　Ⅰ.①鲁…　Ⅱ.①欧…②爱…③曾…　Ⅲ.①英语—汉语—对照读物②诗集—伊朗—中世纪　Ⅳ.①H319.4：I

中国版本图书馆CIP数据核字（2017）第239969号

出版人：	徐　劲
策划编辑：	熊锡源
责任编辑：	熊锡源
封面设计：	曾　斌
责任校对：	林彩云
责任技编：	何雅涛
出版发行：	中山大学出版社
电　　话：	编辑部 020-84110771，84113349，84111997，84110779
	发行部 020-84111998，84111981，84111160
地　　址：	广州市新港西路135号
邮　　编：	510275　　传　真：020-84036565
网　　址：	http://www.zsup.com.cn　E-mail：zdcbs@mail.sysu.edu.cn
印刷者：	广东省农垦总局印刷厂
规　　格：	880mm×1230mm　1/32　4印张　100千字
版次印次：	2017年10月第1版　2017年10月第1次印刷
定　　价：	32.00元

如发现本书因印装质量影响阅读，请与出版社发行部联系调换

欧玛尔·海亚姆（1048—1131）塑像（位于伊朗内沙布尔）

欧玛尔·海亚姆的纪念碑及其内景
(1963年建成,位于伊朗内沙布尔)

译　序

少年时在某本书里读到几句话，大致是：

当你我走到那帘幕之外，
这世界仍将长久地存在。
它眼里，我们到来与离别，
像一粒小石子投进大海。

后来才知道它是波斯诗人欧玛尔·海亚姆的诗，来自《鲁拜集》。这几句话我一直没有忘记，在人生许多时刻，它们时常萦绕在我心头，成为我心灵的一部分。

少年时读《鲁拜集》，只是朦胧地感受到那种略带感伤的优美。如今重又拿起，更认识到它的深邃。翻阅了几个译本，多少有些失望。有的过于晦涩，有的过于激昂，有的还有不少错解。而我心中的"鲁拜"，虽然深刻，但文字上并不艰涩。在情感和节奏上，它应该是平缓悠远的。我曾听过波斯语吟诵的"鲁拜"，似长风流水，有其独特的悠长韵律。《鲁拜集》中涉及不少历史与宗教的背景，包含着丰富的哲学和神学思辨。如果缺少这些方面的知识结构，译文难免有牵强之处。当然，要译好它，最需要的还是那种可遇而不可求的情感的共鸣。于是萌生了一种念头：自己译一本《鲁拜集》，聊以寄情，聊以解忧，略做无用之事，稍遣有涯之生。

对《鲁拜集》的研究，已经有无数的长篇大论，无需在此多费笔墨，但一点粗略的介绍还是必要的。"鲁拜"是波斯语的音译，而波斯语中这一名词又来自阿拉伯语，字根的意思是"四"。波斯语的"鲁拜"是一种两行的短诗，每行又分为两个小句，共四个部分，可以认为是四行诗。每行末尾押韵，或者第一、二、四行押韵，与中国古诗的"绝句"有些相似。萨曼王朝时期，波斯文学之父鲁达基（850—941）就曾创作过大量这样的四行诗。"鲁拜"这个译名缺少字面上的美感，但已是约定俗成的称呼。也有翻译家将之称为"柔巴依""波斯短歌行"等等，但仍以"鲁拜"最广为人知。

欧玛尔·海亚姆（旧译为莪默、奥玛伽音等）1048年生于波斯的内沙布尔（今伊朗东北部）。他生活的年代，正值塞尔柱王朝统治波斯时期。他年轻时曾游学于中亚古城撒马尔罕（今乌兹别克斯坦），并在布哈拉（今乌兹别克斯坦）精研数学与天文。后应塞尔柱王朝苏丹马立克沙赫之邀，前往首都伊斯法罕（今伊朗中部），进入宫廷，担任太医和天文台长。他著有《代数问题的论证》，论及三次方程的几何解法等当时的前沿问题；在几何学方面，他的著述可谓是非欧几何学的源头；他主持编制过天文表，参与历法的改革，制定的"哲拉勒历"比现行的"格里高利历"还要精确。但在苏丹马立克沙赫死后，塞尔柱宫廷政局动荡，新历未能施行，海亚姆的仕宦生涯也多有沉浮。他晚年退居内沙布尔，1131年去世，葬于城郊。

海亚姆生前以学者闻名，诗名并不显赫，也许是因为他在诗中表现出对宗教的怀疑态度，颇不容于当世。去世数十年后才有人在历史著作中提及他写的四行诗。《鲁拜集》现存最早的抄本是1208年的，收录了252首诗，藏于牛津大学图书馆。海亚姆作为诗人的身份，可以说是700多年后英国诗人爱德华·菲兹杰拉德重塑的。

菲兹杰拉德出生于19世纪英国上流社会家庭，毕业于剑桥大学。他从友人爱德华·考威尔（其后成为牛津大学第一位梵语教授）那里得到海亚姆"鲁拜"的抄本，并于1858年完成了第一版的译稿。但他的译诗一开始也没有得到应有的认可，不光投稿无果，连次年自费印刷的小册子也乏人问津。三年后，诗集得到了当时著名诗人斯文伯恩和罗塞蒂的赞赏和评论，但知者甚少。直到1868年第二版发行之后，才赢得广泛的声誉。菲兹杰拉德的翻译并不是直译，而是超越了手稿中零散的语句，将海亚姆四行诗的精神内核和诗意外形在英语中重构成一个连贯流畅、气韵生动的整体,一件充满东方式的哲思与美感的艺术品。借助菲兹杰拉德的神来之笔,《鲁拜集》开始风行文坛,长盛不衰,成为英语文学乃至世界文学的经典,甚至使波斯人得以重新发现这位被长期忽略的诗人。这是文学史上的最奇妙的相遇之一。正如博尔赫斯所说,"死亡、变迁和时间促使一个人了解另一个人,使两人合成一个诗人"。(博尔赫斯:《爱德华·菲茨杰拉尔德之谜》)

这本小书中的一百零一首短诗,和多数中文译本一样,是译自菲兹杰拉德的英文译本(第四版),而不是海亚姆的波斯语原文。不过,仅对这本小书而言,这未必是多大的缺陷。它的本意不在于编撰一部原汁原味的"海亚姆诗选",算不上严格的文学史研究。海亚姆的"鲁拜"曾长期湮没无闻,正是通过菲兹杰拉德的英译本,它才真正进入世界文学的视野,而菲氏的英译本已然是英语文学的经典。海亚姆撒播的是诗歌的种子,它可以生长在波斯语的土壤中,也可以在别的语言中萌蘖,尽管经过一代又一代的译者培育,枝叶花果会有不同,然而,经典之为经典,正是因为它有着超越地域、时代和语言的品质,多一次辗转又有何妨。

由于职业和兴趣,也许今后几年中会有机会系统地学习波斯文,也希望有生之年能够诵读波斯文的"鲁拜",一定会有新的理解。但执着于原文,可能也是一种执念。新的理解也许非关文字，更多是来自对人生的认识和当下的情怀，而这种认识和情怀是流动的。即便有了新的理解，会不会再有机缘和心绪去译一个更好更全的版本，亦不可知。趁着诗情尚未随年华流逝，译一本这样的小书，亦无不可。

《鲁拜集》中有很多优美的元素：美酒与明月、玫瑰与夜莺、水边的花园、荒漠的流泉，等等。它也歌颂那种明快而诗意的生活，比如最常被人引用的第十二首：

> 树荫下摊开那一卷诗章，
> 放一罐葡萄酒，一点干粮，
> 有你在身边来为我吟唱，
> 这荒野已是美好的天堂。

但这样的诗句其实不多。《鲁拜集》并不是一本欢乐的歌谣，歌颂美酒，歌颂享乐，都掩盖不了深刻的忧愁。这种忧愁来自对生命最真切的认识，来自对世界和人生最执着却又最无望的追问，来自不可预知的命运、不可揭示的奥秘、不可挽回的离别和不可避免的死亡。正如奥地利诗人里尔克所说："在那最深奥、最重要的事物上，我们是无名的孤单。"宗教家让人把所有的追问归结为神，用来世的希望去弥除此世的困惑与苦恼。哲学家叫人把所有的追问转化为概念，用抽象的思辨来构建一个更"真实"但也更无趣的本原。最终，它们都使人厌倦。海亚姆这样的诗人，则叫人回归生命的本真。而生命的本真，最鲜明的就是它的无常、它的有限。人能做的，只是在尚属于自己的时光里欢欣沉醉，以真实而绝望的欢乐对抗着不可知的命运和必然的死亡，而不是用宗教的虔诚和哲学的繁琐来束缚仅有的人生。这种主题其实并不鲜见。它广泛地存在于欧洲文艺复兴时期流行的"行乐需及时"（拉丁语 Carpe Diem）主题当中，也存在于中国的《古诗十九首》、王羲之《兰亭集序》、李白《春夜宴从弟桃花园序》等不朽的诗文里。"人生天地间，忽如远行客。斗酒相娱乐，聊厚不为薄。""修短随化，终期于尽。""浮生若梦，为欢几何？"每当重读这些诗文，对《鲁拜集》的感受便更加真切。《鲁拜集》一方面是"来如流水、逝如疾风"的苍凉之感，一方面是欢歌纵酒、及时行乐的豁达之态，这两者之间的张力所构成的诗性空间，足以容纳无数复杂深刻的人生感受，不论是欢欣还是愁苦，消沉还是解脱。

《鲁拜集》已有众多的中文译本，不妨再多一个。这个译本也有自己注重的一些方面。首先是文字。早期的译本多有文白夹杂，晦涩难懂之处甚多；后期的译本又常有文字上的粗糙。这个译本试图用清晰而凝炼的语言，在雅与俗之间取得平衡。其次是韵律。"鲁拜"是格律诗，英译本每行用的是五音步抑扬格，每个诗节的押韵也很严格。虽然不同语言的格律不能照搬，但译这样的诗，押韵是基本的要求，不能译成分行的散文。此外还有节奏。这个译本除了极个别的句子，每行均为十个字，大体上分为四个停顿，以求节奏的整饬和诵读的自然。虽然当前英诗汉译中比较流行的是"以顿代步"的做法，即以诗行中的停顿来代替英文的"音步"，但我认为，"音步"和诵读时的语义停顿不能等同，停顿多了，难免有拖沓之感。也正因这些限制，译诗不能没有缺憾。有些过于复杂的意象和典故，难以在有限的文字空间中充分表现；有些细节的字眼不得不舍弃，以顾全主旨。有些诗节下面，也有必要补充三言两语的解释，对主题、意象或修辞稍作提示，但愿不至于破坏阅读的乐趣。

就这本小书的设计而言，我执意在译诗之后留下数页空白。这几页空白，像是未及填写的生命的卷轴，它提醒着我们人生的有限，也告诉我们尚有时日可以欢歌畅饮，这本是《鲁拜集》自身的主题。正如第二十四首所言：

趁我们未及在土中埋没，

把我们尚有的尽情挥霍。
待复归尘土，就永无美酒，
永无欢歌，也永无那歌者。

　　这几页空白，又像是一面墙壁。每个阅读经典的人，都在面对自身、面对世界与人生提出那些永恒的困惑与追问。每一个能对《鲁拜集》这样的东西产生兴趣的人，在内心深处都是一位面壁者。而答案，只能在有限的个体生命中去寻求。不管这种寻求是否注定无果，寻求的过程所带来的体验，足以丰富我们对于生命的理解。每一个人，都是自己的破壁人。

　　译这本诗集，也是偶然。它更多的是一种个人阅读体验的凝结。它并不意在成为经典。它记录了我生命的一个片段，一段阅读经典、认识自己、理解人生的特殊历程。也许译完了，读过了，自己也会遗忘大半。在时光的长河里，没有什么可以免于衰朽，不论是人，还是文字。如果说有什么期待，只是希望还有人——哪怕只有一个人——从中读到了一两句印象深刻的话，在人生的许多时刻萦绕在心头，成为他精神世界的一部分。仿佛那个少年时代的我。

2017年4月
于中山大学

CONTENTS/目　录

I. /一 ································· 1
II. /二 ································· 2
III. /三 ································· 3
IV. /四 ································· 4
V. /五 ································· 5
VI. /六 ································· 6
VII. /七 ································· 7
VIII. /八 ································· 8
IX. /九 ································· 9
X. /十 ································· 10
XI. /十一 ································· 11
XII. /十二 ································· 12
XIII. /十三 ································· 13
XIV. /十四 ································· 14
XV. /十五 ································· 15
XVI. /十六 ································· 16
XVII. /十七 ································· 17
XVIII. /十八 ································· 18
XIX. /十九 ································· 19
XX. /二十 ································· 20
XXI. /二十一 ································· 21
XXII. /二十二 ································· 22
XXIII. /二十三 ································· 23
XXIV. /二十四 ································· 24
XXV. /二十五 ································· 25

XXVI. ／二十六	26
XXVII. ／二十七	27
XXVIII. ／二十八	28
XXIX. ／二十九	29
XXX. ／三十	30
XXXI. ／三十一	31
XXXII. ／三十二	32
XXXIII. ／三十三	33
XXXIV. ／三十四	34
XXXV. ／三十五	35
XXXVI. ／三十六	36
XXXVII. ／三十七	37
XXXVIII. ／三十八	38
XXXIX. ／三十九	39
XL. ／四十	40
XLI. ／四十一	41
XLII. ／四十二	42
XLIII. ／四十三	43
XLIV. ／四十四	44
XLV. ／四十五	45
XLVI. ／四十六	46
XLVII. ／四十七	47
XLVIII. ／四十八	48
XLIX. ／四十九	49
L. ／五十	50
LI. ／五十一	51
LII. ／五十二	52
LIII. ／五十三	53

LIV. /五十四	54
LV. /五十五	55
LVI. /五十六	56
LVII. /五十七	57
LVIII. /五十八	58
LIX. /五十九	59
LX. /六十	60
LXI. /六十一	61
LXII. /六十二	62
LXIII. /六十三	63
LXIV. /六十四	64
LXV. /六十五	65
LXVI. /六十六	66
LXVII. /六十七	67
LXVIII. /六十八	68
LXIX. /六十九	69
LXX. /七十	70
LXXI. /七十一	71
LXXII. /七十二	72
LXXIII. /七十三	73
LXXIV. /七十四	74
LXXV. /七十五	75
LXXVI. /七十六	76
LXXVII. /七十七	77
LXXVIII. /七十八	78
LXXIX. /七十九	79
LXXX. /八十	80
LXXXI. /八十一	81

LXXXII. ／八十二	82
LXXXIII. ／八十三	83
LXXXIV. ／八十四	84
LXXXV. ／八十五	85
LXXXVI. ／八十六	86
LXXXVII. ／八十七	87
LXXXVIII. ／八十八	88
LXXXIX. ／八十九	89
XC. ／九十	90
XCI. ／九十一	91
XCII. ／九十二	92
XCIII. ／九十三	93
XCIV. ／九十四	94
XCV. ／九十五	95
XCVI. ／九十六	96
XCVII. ／九十七	97
XCVIII. ／九十八	98
XCIX. ／九十九	99
C. ／一百	100
CI. ／一百零一	101

I.

WAKE! For the Sun who scatter'd into flight
The Stars before him from the Field of Night,
Drives Night along with them from Heav'n, and strikes
The Sultan's Turret with a Shaft of Light.

一

醒来吧!红日已经从天园
把黑夜连群星一并驱散。
阳光已把它金色的箭矢
射上了苏丹的塔楼之巅!

II.

Before the phantom of False morning died,
Methought a Voice within the Tavern cried,
"When all the Temple is prepared within,
Why nods the drowsy Worshiper outside?"

二

晨曦的昏昧尚未及散尽,
酒馆中依稀听到了呼声:
"寺院的晨祷已准备妥当,
礼拜者竟在外昏睡不醒?"

  清真寺在召唤人们去做祈祷,然而下一首却说,人们纷纷挤进酒馆而非寺院。

III.

And, as the Cock crew, those who stood before
The Tavern shouted— "Open then the Door!"
"You know how little while we have to stay,
And, once departed, may return no more."

三

雄鸡已报晓,酒馆的门前
拥挤的众人在高声叫喊:
"开门!我们只能欢饮片刻,
一旦离去,就再不能复返。"

  比起少人问津的寺院,酒馆门口却热闹非凡。欢饮片刻,一去不返,喻人生之短暂。

IV.

Now the New Year reviving old Desires,
The thoughtful Soul to Solitude retires,
Where the WHITE HAND OF MOSES on the Bough
Puts out, and Jesus from the Ground suspires.

四

新岁把旧年的欲望唤起,
沉思的心在孤独中隐匿。
穆萨的白手伸上了枝头,
尔撒的呼吸透出了地底。

万物复苏的景象,寓意心灵的苏醒。

　　穆萨和尔撒用的是伊斯兰文化中的名称。穆萨的白手:穆萨即摩西。《旧约·出埃及记》中,神向摩西显现,使他的手变为雪白,以显示神迹。此处"穆萨的白手"是隐喻,某种白色的花朵。尔撒即耶稣。"尔撒的呼吸"也是隐喻,寓意生命、生机。

V.

Iram indeed is gone with all his Rose,
And Jamshyd's Sev'n-ring'd Cup where no one knows;
But still a Ruby kindles in the Vine,
And many a Garden by the Water blows.

五

伊兰城倾圮，玫瑰也消逝；
七环杯埋没，又何处寻觅？
藤间的葡萄却亮如玛瑙，
水边的园中仍鲜花如织。

  宏伟的城市和稀世珍宝都已埋没，当下的生活却是鲜活的。

  伊兰城是传说中阿拉伯半岛南部沙漠中一座消逝的古城。据《古兰经》说，城市中有巍峨的高楼，因城中人拒斥先知胡德而被真主用沙暴所毁。有译本说是波斯花园名，即伊兰花园，位于设拉子。但此园建于十三世纪中叶，晚于海亚姆时期。"杰姆西王的七环杯"，杰姆西王是波斯传说中丕什达德王朝的第四任君王，据传在位三百年，有诸多创造，是文明的缔造者，葡萄酒的发现也与他有关。他有七环宝杯，装着长生之酒。丕什达德王朝和第九首注释提到的凯扬王朝均是传说中的古王朝，不是信史。

VI.

And David's lips are lockt; but in divine
High-piping Pehlevi, with "Wine! Wine! Wine!
"Red Wine!" —the Nightingale cries to the Rose
That sallow cheek of hers t'incarnadine.

六

大卫的歌唇被死亡紧锁，
夜莺却用巴列维语欢歌：
"酒哟——酒哟——红酒哟——"，
唱得玫瑰的脸泛起酡色。

  大卫，古犹太国君主，善弹竖琴作歌，《旧约·诗篇》有多篇传说是他所作。巴列维语，又称钵罗钵语、帕拉维语，3—10世纪的中古波斯语，萨珊帝国的主要语言。此处"Pehlevi"有拟声意味。

VII.

Come, fill the Cup, and in the fire of Spring
Your Winter garment of Repentance fling:
The Bird of Time has but a little way
To flutter—and the Bird is on the Wing.

七

来,满饮此杯!趁融融春阳,
快抛却你那忏悔的冬装。
时间的飞鸟本就难远徙,
何况它早已在悄然飞翔。

  时间的飞鸟难以飞远,喻生命之短。

VIII.

Whether at Naishapur or Babylon,
Whether the Cup with sweet or bitter run,
The Wine of Life keeps oozing drop by drop,
The Leaves of Life keep falling one by one.

八

不论在内沙布或巴比伦,
不论杯中酒酸涩或甘醇,
生命的酒浆正滴滴渗漏,
生命的绿叶正片片凋零。

  不论身在何处,不论幸福还是痛苦,时光和生命都在悄悄流逝。
  内沙布,即内沙布尔,伊朗东部呼罗珊地区的古城。海亚姆生于此,葬于此。

IX.

Each Morn a thousand Roses brings, you say;
Yes, but where leaves the Rose of Yesterday?
And this first Summer month that brings the Rose
Shall take Jamshyd and Kaikobad away.

九

每个清晨都有玫瑰千枝,
昨日的玫瑰又何处寻觅?
滋生玫瑰的初夏,也带走
杰姆西王和凯克白大帝。

  固一世之雄也,而今安在?
  凯克白,传说中凯扬王朝(Kayanian Dynasty)的缔造者。

X.

Well, let it take them! What have we to do
With Kaikobad the Great, or Kaikhosru?
Let Zal and Rustum bluster as they will,
Or Hatim call to Supper—heed not you.

十

带走吧！他们又与我何干？
查尔、鲁什坦，且由其征战，
凯克白或凯霍苏尽管伟大，
哈迪姆召以盛筵，也不管！

　　凯霍苏，凯克白之孙，传说中凯扬王朝第三任君主。郭沫若译本误以为是灭巴比伦、释放犹太奴隶的君主，实际上灭巴比伦的是之后的阿契美尼德王朝——即波斯第一帝国的居鲁士二世。查尔为波斯史诗中的英雄，鲁什坦为其子。哈迪姆也是波斯传说中的英雄，以慷慨闻名。

XI.

With me along the strip of Herbage strown
That just divides the desert from the sown,
Where name of Slave and Sultan is forgot—
And Peace to Mahmud on his golden Throne!

十一

请随我走过这一片草场,
荒漠和良田隔在它两旁。
奴隶与苏丹都已被忘却,
安息吧,金座上的马穆德王。

  萋萋荒草,隔开良田荒漠,如墓园隔开人间与死后。君主与奴隶,已再无分别。

  马穆德(971—1030)为加兹尼王朝第二任君主,武功赫赫。王朝疆域覆盖北印度、阿富汗、花剌子模和波斯。"苏丹"作为君主头衔,自他而始。

XII.

A Book of Verses underneath the Bough,
A Jug of Wine, a Loaf of Bread—and Thou
Beside me singing in the Wilderness—
Oh, Wilderness were Paradise enow!

十二

树荫下摊开那一卷诗章,
放一罐葡萄酒,一点干粮,
有你在身边来为我吟唱,
这荒野已是美好的天堂。

XIII.

Some for the Glories of This World; and some
Sigh for the Prophet's Paradise to come;
Ah, take the Cash, and let the Credit go,
Nor heed the rumble of a distant Drum!

十三

有人追求的是此世荣光,
有人指望先知说的天堂。
且拿好现钱,别要那债券,
别理会远处隆隆的鼓响。

  鼓声指天堂之鼓。现钱指今世的快乐,债券指天堂中才能兑现的幸福。不要把希望寄托在天堂。

XIV.

Look to the blowing Rose about us— "Lo,
Laughing," she says, "into the world I blow,
At once the silken tassel of my Purse
Tear, and its Treasure on the Garden throw."

十四

你看那周边玫瑰多绚烂,
她在说:"我笑着来到世间。
一旦锦囊的丝穗被扯断,
囊中的珍宝就洒遍花园。"

  囊中的珍宝比喻花谢时花瓣纷飞。叹花期之短,如人生之短。

XV.

And those who husbanded the Golden grain,
And those who flung it to the winds like Rain,
Alike to no such aureate Earth are turn'd
As, buried once, Men want dug up again.

十五

勤劳者种出金色的谷粒,
奢靡者将金粒挥洒如雨。
他们死后都化不成金泥,
又有谁愿意将浊土挖取?

贫贱富贵,死后均化为污泥浊土。

XVI.

The Worldly Hope men set their Hearts upon
Turns Ashes—or it prospers; and anon,
Like Snow upon the Desert's dusty Face,
Lighting a little hour or two—was gone.

十六

寄托在此世的希望易灭，
或许繁盛一时，旋即消解。
它们只闪过片刻的光辉，
像大漠黄沙上那层薄雪。

XVII.

Think, in this batter'd Caravanserai
Whose Portals are alternate Night and Day,
How Sultan after Sultan with his Pomp
Abode his destin'd Hour, and went his way.

十七

世界不过是残破的旅店,
昼夜的交替,如柴扉开关。
多少苏丹和他们的荣华,
只稍稍驻留,旋即又走远。

再伟大的君主,也是天地间的匆匆过客。

如读李白《春夜宴从弟桃花园序》:"夫天地者,万物之逆旅;光阴者,百代之过客。"又如读《古诗十九首》其三:"人生天地间,忽如远行客。"

XVIII.

They say the Lion and the Lizard keep
The courts where Jamshyd gloried and drank deep:
And Bahram, that great Hunter—the Wild Ass
Stamps o'er his Head, but cannot break his Sleep.

十八

杰姆西王曾宴饮的宫殿,
惟野狮和蜥蜴逡巡其间。
野驴踏过巴朗姆的陵墓,
惊不醒这"好猎王"的长眠。

　　巴朗姆五世为波斯萨珊王朝(224—651 年)的君主,420—438 年在位,好田猎。

XIX.

I sometimes think that never blows so red
The Rose as where some buried Caesar bled;
That every Hyacinth the Garden wears
Dropt in her Lap from some once lovely Head.

十九

我想，帝王埋骨处的玫瑰
定是开得比别处更艳美，
园中每一丛风信子，定是
从当年的美人头上飘坠。

　　帝王美人皆尘土，园中的鲜花，又是尘土化育。

XX.

And this reviving Herb whose tender Green
Fledges the River-Lip on which we lean—
Ah, lean upon it lightly! for who knows
From what once lovely Lip it springs unseen!

二十

复苏的春草新羽般柔嫩,
我们倚靠着河流的绿唇。
轻些倚吧,谁知道这春草
是昔日多美的嘴唇滋生?

  "河流的绿唇"指"河岸"。谁知草下的泥土中曾埋着生前多美的人,成为春草的养分?

XXI.

Ah, my Beloved, fill the Cup that clears
TO-DAY of past Regret and future Fears:
To-morrow—Why, To-morrow I may be
Myself with Yesterday's Sev'n thousand Years.

二十一

我的爱人哪,再满饮此杯,
一解昨日之悔,明日之畏!
明日,明日之我或已变回
七千年前那混沌的土灰。

　　"七千年前":按波斯传说,世界始于七千年前。这里为回归尘土之意。

XXII.

For some we loved, the loveliest and the best
That from his Vintage rolling Time hath prest,
Have drunk their Cup a Round or two before,
And one by one crept silently to rest.

二十二

我们深爱的美好的人物
也被滚滚时光碾成酒汁——
他们只欢饮了一场两场，
就已黯然离去，长睡不起。

时光碾过世人，如酿酒师碾压葡萄。

XXIII.

And we, that now make merry in the Room
They left, and Summer dresses in new bloom,
  Ourselves must we beneath the Couch of Earth
Descend—ourselves to make a Couch—for whom?

二十三

我们欢会在前人的华堂,
仲夏用繁花做它的盛装。
  不久将埋在大地之床下,
自身又化作了谁人之床?

XXIV.

Ah, make the most of what we yet may spend,
Before we too into the Dust descend;
Dust into Dust, and under Dust, to lie,
Sans Wine, sans Song, sans Singer, and—sans End!

二十四

趁我们未及在土中埋没,
把我们尚有的尽情挥霍。
待复归尘土,就永无美酒,
永无欢歌,也永无那歌者。

XXV.

Alike for those who for TO-DAY prepare,
And those that after some TO-MORROW stare,
A Muezzin from the Tower of Darkness cries,
"Fools! your Reward is neither Here nor There."

二十五

有些人盼望今日的报偿,
有些人期待来日的奖赏。
司祷在黑暗的塔楼高叫:
"愚人!那报赏本就无望!"

　　清真寺宣礼塔上传来司祷者领诵之声,诗人却仿佛从中听出了不同的含义,听出了虚无与无望。

XXVI.

Why, all the Saints and Sages who discuss'd
Of the Two Worlds so wisely—they are thrust
Like foolish Prophets forth; their Words to Scorn
Are scatter'd, and their Mouths are stopt with Dust.

二十六

贤哲们高谈天堂和今世,
如愚蠢的预言者被厌弃。
他们的言语沦为了笑柄,
他们的嘴终被尘土封闭。

所谓圣徒和智者,自以为掌握真理,侃侃而谈,却不知自身迂腐可笑,一样要归于尘土。

XXVII.

Myself when young did eagerly frequent
Doctor and Saint, and heard great argument
About it and about: but evermore
Came out by the same door where in I went.

二十七

年青时我遍访智者、圣人，
听他们说那些堂皇高论。
却依然从他们身边离去，
走出来时所入的那扇门。

　　智者与圣徒讲述的大道理，并未能解开人生的谜题，故失望而返。

XXVIII.

With them the seed of Wisdom did I sow,
And with mine own hand wrought to make it grow;
And this was all the Harvest that I reap'd—
"I came like Water, and like Wind I go."

二十八

随贤哲我播下智慧之种，
又亲手培育至繁茂葱茏。
而今我所得的全部收获，
只是"来如流水，逝如疾风"。

XXIX.

Into this Universe, and Why not knowing
Nor Whence, like Water willy-nilly flowing;
And out of it, as Wind along the Waste,
I know not Whither, willy-nilly blowing.

二十九

我如流水般进入了宇宙，
不知何来，也不知何由。
又如荒漠之风飘离世间，
不知何往，也不能停留。

XXX.

What, without asking, hither hurried Whence?
And, without asking, Whither hurried hence!
Oh, many a Cup of this forbidden Wine
Must drown the memory of that insolence!

三十

再莫问我因何来到此地，
再莫问我终向何处归去。
且畅饮这被禁绝的美酒，
来淹没那些愤懑的愁绪。

XXXI.

Up from Earth's Center through the Seventh Gate
I rose, and on the Throne of Saturn sate,
And many a Knot unravel'd by the Road;
But not the Master-knot of Human Fate.

三十一

从地心直升至第七天门,
在土星宝座上暂时栖身,
沿途我解开无数的谜团,
命运的奥秘却终不可闻。

　　上穷碧落下黄泉,在茫茫宇宙中探寻终极的奥秘,但命运之谜终不可解。

　　古代天文学将第七层天空称为"土星天","地心说"和初期的"日心说"都是如此。

XXXII.

There was the Door to which I found no Key;
There was the Veil through which I might not see:
Some little talk awhile of ME and THEE
There was—and then no more of THEE and ME.

三十二

这是我无从开启的门户,
这是我无法窥透的帘幕。
只一时听闻"我""你"之辨,
随后"你"与"我"又沉寂如初。

　　这是《鲁拜集》中较为晦涩的一首。"我"与"你"的关系,是人与神的关系。短暂、个体的人对代表永恒、整体的神的追寻与发问,而这种对话又因人的短暂而只能存在一时。

XXXIII.

Earth could not answer; nor the Seas that mourn
In flowing Purple, of their Lord Forlorn;
Nor rolling Heaven, with all his Signs reveal'd
And hidden by the sleeve of Night and Morn.

三十三

大地喑哑;海洋沉默不言,
空自披着它哀悼的紫衫;
旋转的天空也无从回答,
任朝夕把星宫显露、遮掩。

　　　天地万物都沉默不语,无法给出关于终极问题的答案。

XXXIV.

Then of the THEE IN ME who works behind
The Veil, I lifted up my hands to find
A lamp amid the Darkness; and I heard,
As from Without— "THE ME WITHIN THEE BLIND!"

三十四

我向幕后的"我中你"叩问,
如同摸索黑暗中的孤灯,
有一个声音从空无传来:
"那'你中之我'本就是盲人。"

　　"我中你"指的是"心中的神"。向帘幕后不可知的神发问,如同在黑暗中寻求光明。但神说,自己也是盲目的,不能给出什么指引。

XXXV.

Then to the Lip of this poor earthen Urn
I lean'd, the Secret of my Life to learn:
And Lip to Lip it murmur'd— "While you live,
"Drink! —for, once dead, you never shall return."

三十五

我俯身凑近这陶瓷唇边,
想要探解我生命的幽玄。
它贴着我的唇轻声低语:
"生时当畅饮,死后不得返!"

  神不给答案,酒似乎可以。生命的幽玄似乎也很简单,就是在短暂的生命里及时行乐。

XXXVI.

I think the Vessel, that with fugitive
Articulation answer'd, once did live,
And drink; and Ah! the passive Lip I kiss'd,
How many Kisses might it take—and give!

三十六

我想,这对我低语的陶瓮,
也曾活在世间,也曾畅饮——
我吻的这冷却的唇,也曾
受过多少吻,吻过多少人。

  陶瓮是泥土所制,泥土是逝者所化,陶罐中似有逝去的生命。第三十七首也是此意。

XXXVII.

For I remember stopping by the way
To watch a Potter thumping his wet Clay:
And with its all-obliterated Tongue
It murmur'd— "Gently, Brother, gently, pray!"

三十七

昔时我曾在旅途中驻足，
见陶匠奋力夯捣着陶土。
那土用古老的语言低吟：
"轻些吧，兄弟，难忍这捶杵——"

XXXVIII.

And has not such a Story from of Old
Down Man's successive generations roll'd
Of such a clod of saturated Earth
Cast by the Maker into Human mold?

三十八

那故事从远古流传至今，
被一代又一代的人深信：
从那团潮湿的黏土之中，
造物主塑出了人的身形。

XXXIX.

And not a drop that from our Cups we throw
For Earth to drink of, but may steal below
To quench the fire of Anguish in some Eye
There hidden—far beneath, and long ago.

三十九

酹洒大地的每一粒酒珠，
都悄然渗透到地底深处，
去滋润深埋已久的逝者，
把他们焦灼的眼眸安抚。

　　土中埋着逝者，渴望着美酒与生命。

XL.

As then the Tulip for her morning sup
Of Heav'nly Vintage from the soil looks up,
Do you devoutly do the like, till Heav'n
To Earth invert you—like an empty Cup.

四十

郁金香从土中仰望天堂,
举杯承接着朝饮的琼浆。
你可一样虔诚,直到上天
将你如空杯倒扣在地上?

　　空杯之说可参照第一百零一首。空杯扣地,如生命终止。

XLI.

Perplext no more with Human or Divine,
To-morrow's tangle to the winds resign,
And lose your fingers in the tresses of
The Cypress-slender Minister of Wine.

四十一

莫困扰于"人"与"神"的谜题,
把明日之忧在风中抛去。
酒仙的身姿秀颀如翠柏,
等你抚弄它柔软的发丝。

XLII.

And if the Wine you drink, the Lip you press,
End in what All begins and ends in—Yes;
Think then you are TO-DAY what YESTERDAY
You were—TO-MORROW you shall not be less.

四十二

若是杯中的酒、杯边的唇,
终回到万物生灭的根本,
今日之我本是昨日之我,
明日之身何异今日之身?

　　"万物生灭的根本",指尘土。万物一体,死生一如,无非尘土。

XLIII.

So when the Angel of the darker Drink
At last shall find you by the river-brink,
And, offering his Cup, invite your Soul
Forth to your Lips to quaff—you shall not shrink.

四十三

因此，若黑暗酒乡的天使
终在河水之滨与你相遇，
递上酒杯，邀出你的灵魂，
你当一饮而尽，切莫退避。

死亡来时，不需要恐惧，也许意味着灵魂的解脱与自由。

XLIV.

Why, if the Soul can fling the Dust aside,
And naked on the Air of Heaven ride,
 Wer't not a Shame—were't not a Shame for him
In this clay carcass crippled to abide?

四十四

若灵魂能抛却躯壳之重，
裸身在天国中冯虚御风，
 难道它不会感受到耻辱——
曾委顿在这泥土的壳中？

XLV.

'Tis but a Tent where takes his one day's rest
A Sultan to the realm of Death addrest;
The Sultan rises, and the dark Ferrash
Strikes, and prepares it for another Guest.

四十五

这只是苏丹临时的帐幕,
他奔赴冥界时在此短驻。
他一走,天奴就将之收卷,
等有后来者再重新搭树。

  参见第十七首。天空如暂时的营帐,人生是奔赴冥界的旅程,伟大的君王亦是如此。

XLVI.

And fear not lest Existence closing your
Account, and mine, should know the like no more;
The Eternal Saki from that Bowl has pour'd
Millions of Bubbles like us, and will pour.

四十六

莫怕"存在"终将你我勾销,
你我的逝去它很快忘掉。
万千酒沫曾迸灭在盏中,
永恒的侍酒仍不断斟倒。

  在永恒的"存在"眼中,人如酒中之沫,不断迸灭,新的泡沫又不断产生。

XLVII.

When You and I behind the Veil are past,
Oh, but the long, long while the World shall last,
Which of our Coming and Departure heeds
As the Sea's self should heed a pebble-cast.

四十七

当你我走到那帘幕之外,
这世界仍将长久地存在。
它眼里,我们到来与离别,
像一粒小石子投进大海。

帘幕喻生死之界限。在宏大的宇宙中,在神的眼里,个人的生死离别太过渺小。

XLVIII.

A Moment's Halt—a momentary taste
Of BEING from the Well amid the Waste—
And Lo!—the phantom Caravan has reacht
The NOTHING it set out from—Oh, make haste!

四十八

在荒漠清泉边稍稍停驻,
只片刻得饮"存在"之甘露。
快饮吧!可叹那一队幽影,
才走出"虚无",又复归"虚无"。

  荒漠中驼队的意象,从远方而来,又消逝在远方,如人之生于虚无,转瞬又复归虚无。只片刻得以啜饮"存在"之泉,喻生命之短暂。

XLIX.

Would you that spangle of Existence spend
About THE SECRET—quick about it, Friend!
A Hair perhaps divides the False from True—
And upon what, prithee, does life depend?

四十九

朋友,若你定要空耗时日,
执意探寻那终极的奥秘——
真与伪不过是一线之隔,
试问哪边是人生的依据?

寻找终极的答案,分清哪些是幻像,哪些是本真——或曰人的终极关怀、形而上的思索,不过是徒劳的。最终或许不得不求助于神学,如下几节所言。下几节虽着力铺陈神之伟大,实为铺垫,暗含嘲讽。找到了世界的本质,并不等于找到人生的意义。

L.

A Hair perhaps divides the False and True;
Yes; and a single Alif were the clue—
Could you but find it—to the Treasure-house,
And peradventure to THE MASTER too;

五十

真与伪或许只隔着一线,
欲辨之,需回溯万物本源。
追寻它你或能渐入宝藏,
宇宙的主宰也或可得见。

  原文第二行字面意思是"让'阿里夫'来引导"。"阿里夫"为阿拉伯文的首字母。追随"阿里夫",是追寻万物本源之义。在宗教中追溯的结果,就是神。基督教《新约·启示录》(22:13)中上帝自称:"我是'阿尔法',我是'欧米伽';是首先的,也是末后的;是开始,也是终结。"——从希腊文首字母到末字母,比喻上帝是一切之起始与终结,可为参照。

LI.

Whose secret Presence through Creation's veins
Running Quicksilver-like eludes your pains;
Taking all shapes from Mah to Mahi and
They change and perish all—but He remains;

五十一

宇宙的主宰深藏于玄冥，
造化之伟力，可抚慰你心。
品物流形，皆变换且消逝，
永存不变者，唯有此神灵。

　　言神之伟大与永恒。

LII.

A moment guessed—then back behind the Fold
Immerst of Darkness round the Drama roll'd
Which, for the Pastime of Eternity,
He doth Himself contrive, enact, behold.

五十二

神只显露一瞬,旋即不见,
他的戏台边萦回着黑暗。
他有无穷的时间要消磨,
只能自排自演,独自观看。

　　"戏台"喻宇宙与人世,神主宰着舞台上的一切。人千辛万苦寻到了神,但神似乎忙碌得很,也孤独得很,也未能回答人的追问。寻求宇宙的形而上本质,并不能解决有限人生的意义问题。

LIII.

But if in vain, down on the stubborn floor
Of Earth, and up to Heav'n's unopening Door,
You gaze TO-DAY, while You are You—how then
TO-MORROW, when You shall be You no more?

五十三

倘若，你只能站在这地上，
徒劳地仰望紧闭的天堂——
今日有此身，你尚可观瞻，
明日身已丧，又用何参详？

  以有限之身，究无穷之事，岂非过于执着？如果形而上的求索只是徒劳，又当如何？从此节开始，复归当下，也复归消沉。

LIV.

Waste not your Hour, nor in the vain pursuit
Of This and That endeavor and dispute;
Better be jocund with the fruitful Grape
Than sadden after none, or bitter, Fruit.

五十四

切勿再空费宝贵的时辰，
执着于此是彼非的空论！
与其戚戚于无果或苦果，
何如把丰美的酒浆畅饮？

  与其探玄，不如饮酒。

LV.

You know, my Friends, with what a brave Carouse
I made a Second Marriage in my house;
Divorced old barren Reason from my Bed,
And took the Daughter of the Vine to Spouse.

五十五

朋友啊，今日我再度洞房，
宅中办着婚筵，好大排场！
我休掉"理性"这不孕老妻，
娶了"葡萄之女"来做新娘！

　　"葡萄之女"为"葡萄酒"。酒醉欢谑之感跃然纸上。苦思而无果，何如飞觞而醉月。拼却醉颜红，一解千千结。

LVI.

For "Is" and "Is-not" though with Rule and Line,
And "UP-AND-DOWN" by Logic I define,
Of all that one should care to fathom, I
was never deep in anything but—Wine.

五十六

我能用几何证明伪与真,
也能用逻辑推演神与人。
但世人所欲之一切学问,
除了酒道,我都涉之不深。

　　算术几何的学问,可以区分命题之真伪;神学不同于信教,需要逻辑思辨来推演形而上的层面。海亚姆是大学者,精通数学、天文、神学,但在他眼中,理性的思辨使人厌倦,唯有在饮酒作乐之中放纵沉沦,似近于人生真谛。

LVII.

Ah, by my Computations, People say,
Reduce the Year to better reckoning?—Nay,
'Twas only striking from the Calendar
Unborn To-morrow and dead Yesterday.

五十七

众人皆称赞我精于数算，
能修正旧历，使之更精简。
不知我只从历法中删去
未生的明日，已死的昨天。

  海亚姆是天文学家，曾修正历法。但诗人自称，修改历法并不足道。他自己生命的历法，删去明日和昨天，只剩下今朝。昨日之日不可留，明日之日多烦忧，今日之日，不妨欢歌纵酒。

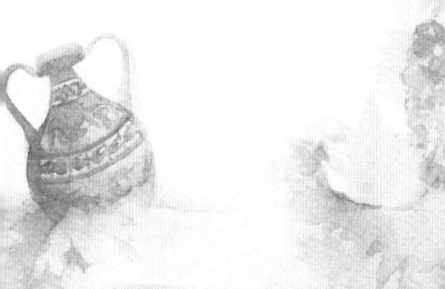

LVIII.

And lately, by the Tavern Door agape,
Came shining through the Dusk an Angel Shape
Bearing a Vessel on his Shoulder; and
He bid me taste of it; and 'twas—the Grape!

五十八

某日黄昏,店门尚未掩上,
有天使降临,闪耀着光芒。
他肩扛陶樽,让我来品鉴,
樽中赫然是葡萄的佳酿!

　　伊斯兰教兴起后逐渐禁酒。此节称酒为天使的馈赠,后数节又大赞酒之神奇,乃神之恩赐,颇为离经叛道。

LIX.

The Grape that can with Logic absolute
The Two-and-Seventy jarring Sects confute:
The sovereign Alchemist that in a trice
Life's leaden metal into Gold transmute;

五十九

美酒啊，它以绝对的高论，
压倒七十二教派的纷争。
它还是至高的炼金术师，
让生命的铅块瞬间成金！

　　美酒讲的道理，才是无可辩驳的道理。它的魔力，是化腐朽为神奇的魔力。

LX.

The mighty Mahmud, Allah-breathing Lord,
That all the misbelieving and black Horde
Of Fears and Sorrows that infest the Soul
Scatters before him with his whirlwind Sword.

六十

它是马穆德,神佑之雄主!
把信邪的群寇纷纷驱逐——
侵蚀人心的恐惧和悲痛,
被他旋风之剑一举扫除。

  马穆德,见第十一首注释。此节称颂酒的威力,横扫一切忧愁愤懑。

LXI.

Why, be this Juice the growth of God, who dare
Blaspheme the twisted tendril as a Snare?
A Blessing, we should use it, should we not?
And if a Curse—why, then, Who set it there?

六十一

若酒浆取自真主的滋养,
葡萄藤的柔须怎是罗网?
若是福,何不去尽情消受?
若是祸,谁让它来到世上?

  酒浆产自葡萄,葡萄是真主创世所制,是真主的恩赐。若卫道士诅咒葡萄酒,岂非对真主不敬?

LXII.

I must abjure the Balm of Life, I must,
Scared by some After-reckoning ta'en on trust,
Or lured with Hope of some Diviner Drink,
To fill the Cup—when crumbled into Dust!

六十二

我要把生命的琼浆戒除——
或畏惧死后惩罚的痛苦；
或期待天堂有仙酒盈杯——
但只能等到我复归尘土！

　　酒这辈子是戒不掉了。沉湎于美酒，有违教义，死后当受严惩；而伊斯兰此世禁酒，但天堂可有醇酒为伴。地狱的刑罚和天堂的诱惑，仍不足使诗人断绝此世畅饮之欢愉，在复归尘土之前，仍要纵酒欢歌。原诗所谓"更神圣的酒浆斟满杯盏"，也是隐喻，指天堂中永恒的生命和享乐。

LXIII.

Of threats of Hell and Hopes of Paradise!
One thing at least is certain—This Life flies;
One thing is certain and the rest is Lies;
The Flower that once has blown forever dies.

六十三

地狱的残酷? 天堂的希望?
唯一确定者,是此生易丧。
只此为真,其余无非谎言!
花开只一时,便永远凋亡。

宗教的说教,是关于虚无缥缈的地狱、天堂,遥不可知。而人生的短暂却满眼皆是,比地狱天堂更真实。

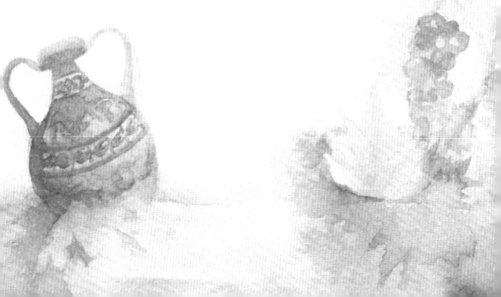

LXIV.

Strange, is it not? that of the myriads who
Before us pass'd the door of Darkness through,
Not one returns to tell us of the Road,
Which to discover we must travel too.

六十四

奇怪的是，之前有千万人
已然穿过那幽暗的大门。
却再无一人从那里回转，
为你我讲述这必然旅程。

LXV.

The Revelations of Devout and Learn'd
Who rose before us, and as Prophets burn'd,
Are all but Stories, which, awoke from Sleep
They told their comrades, and to Sleep return'd.

六十五

有多少虔信或博学之士,
宣扬的天启不过是故事。
他们只是从长眠中醒来,
告知了你我,又沉沉睡去。

  诸多圣贤大哲,自认得到天启,其实不过是痴人说梦。

LXVI.

I sent my Soul through the Invisible,
Some letter of that After-life to spell:
And by and by my Soul return'd to me,
And answer'd "I Myself am Heav'n and Hell!"

六十六

我把灵魂派往未知之地,
想稍稍探知那死后之世。
等到灵魂渐渐回转,它说:
所谓地狱、天堂,是你自己!

LXVII.

Heav'n but the Vision of fulfill'd Desire,
And Hell the Shadow from a Soul on fire
Cast on the Darkness into which Ourselves,
So late emerg'd from, shall so soon expire.

六十七

天堂是欲望满足的憧憬,
地狱是灵魂焦灼的阴影,
投射在无尽的黑暗之上——
人,才从中生,又向其消隐。

　　天堂与地狱,是人的希望和痛苦所生出的幻景。人生于黑暗,复归于黑暗。如前诗第四十八首所言,生于虚无,复归于虚无。

LXVIII.

We are no other than a moving row
Of Magic Shadow-shapes that come and go
Round with the Sun-illumin'd Lantern held
In Midnight by the Master of the Show.

六十八

我们是幻术炮制的幽影,
围着那点亮光匆匆行进。
那灯笼乃是用太阳点亮,
被幻术师夜半提在掌心。

  以魔术师喻神。此节开始,一连串的比喻,来阐述神与人之间的关系,言神之掌控一切,人之渺小无力。

LXIX.

But helpless Pieces of the Game He plays
Upon this Chequer-board of Nights and Days;
Hither and thither moves, and checks, and slays,
And one by one back in the Closet lays.

六十九

人不过是神摆弄的棋子，
棋盘的黑白，是昼夜交替。
任你纵横捭阖，或擒或杀，
棋局终结时就收回匣里。

  以棋手喻神。

LXX.

The Ball no question makes of Ayes and Noes,
But Here or There as strikes the Player goes;
And He that toss'd you down into the Field,
He knows about it all—HE knows—HE knows!

七十

皮球能有什么从与不从,
只能由球手来任意抛弄。
他何以将你抛进这场地?
一切的缘由,只有他才懂。

以球手喻神。

LXXI.

The Moving Finger writes; and, having writ,
Moves on: nor all your Piety nor Wit
Shall lure it back to cancel half a Line,
Nor all your Tears wash out a Word of it.

七十一

那手指且只顾匆匆奋笔,
写下的章句再不可更易。
任你虔诚机智,难销半行;
任你倾尽眼泪,难洗一字。

  以手指喻神,写下的是不可更改的命运。人的智慧、虔诚或者痛苦,无法改变神的意志和既定的命运。如此,虔信何益,悲哀何益?

LXXII.

And that inverted Bowl they call the Sky,
Whereunder crawling coop'd we live and die,
Lift not your hands to It for help—for It
As impotently moves as you or I.

七十二

那倒扣的大碗人称天空,
从生到死,人们匍匐其中。
再莫要举手向它去求祈,
它无力行动,和我们相同。

向苍天求告,毫无用处。

LXXIII.

With Earth's first Clay They did the Last Man knead,
And there of the Last Harvest sow'd the Seed:
And the first Morning of Creation wrote
What the Last Dawn of Reckoning shall read.

七十三

最后之人来自太初之土,
最后收成来自太初之谷。
创世之初已写就的一切,
审判日的清晨仍要诵读。

   一切早已写就,一切早已注定。

LXXIV.

YESTERDAY This Day's Madness did prepare;
TO-MORROW's Silence, Triumph, or Despair:
Drink! for you not know whence you came, nor why:
Drink! for you know not why you go, nor where.

七十四

昨日已备下今日的颠狂、
明日的沉默、欣喜和绝望。
饮吧！谁知何所来，何所去，
亦不知何故来，何故往！

　　　既已注定，不如纵饮。

LXXV.

I tell you this—When, started from the Goal,
Over the flaming shoulders of the Foal
Of Heav'n Parwin and Mushtari they flung,
In my predestin'd Plot of Dust and Soul.

七十五

告诉你吧,我出生的时日,
木星和七女星团,被抛掷
在太阳这匹火驹的两肩,
在星相已注定的此生里——

　　此节未完,与下一节应连在一起读。此节讲星相,言诗人出生之时,太阳位于金牛座的昴宿星团——即七女星团——和木星之间。星相上有何含义,未及细究,但显然与命运、性格有关。无非是说,此生在出生那一刻已然注定,为醉酒欢歌、放浪形骸寻找托词。原文"此生"前还有"土与魂"的意义:神抟土造人,用呼吸赋予灵魂,"生而为人"的意思。

LXXVI.

The Vine had struck a fiber: which about
It clings my Being—let the Dervish flout;
Of my Base metal may be filed a Key
That shall unlock the Door he howls without.

七十六

葡萄已扎根在我的形骸，
苦行僧的嘲弄，何必见怪？
我这废材能铸成把钥匙，
开门直入——他却徘徊门外。

  命中注定与葡萄美酒为伴，任由卫道士蹙眉。醉中豁然开朗，如通大道。

LXXVII.

And this I know: whether the one True Light
Kindle to Love, or Wrath consume me quite,
One Flash of It within the Tavern caught
Better than in the Temple lost outright.

七十七

那唯一的真火，可以点起
情爱或愤恨，来将我销蚀。
但在酒馆灯火里瞥见它，
却胜过在寺院彷徨迷失。

  那真理或生命的火种，化作种种形态，只有酒馆的灯火似乎最为亲切，最为真实。

LXXVIII.

What! out of senseless Nothing to provoke
A conscious Something to resent the yoke
Of unpermitted Pleasure, under pain
Of Everlasting Penalties, if broke!

七十八

什么？他从无知觉的"无"里
能造出有思想的我和你——
还会怨恨他把欢乐禁锢，
用永恒的刑罚惩处违逆？

  此节开始，有数节是对神的质疑，神做的这些自我矛盾的事，对人有何恩？对宗教宣传的反驳和不屑。

LXXIX.

What! from his helpless Creature be repaid
Pure Gold for what he lent him dross-allay'd—
 Sue for a Debt we never did contract,
And cannot answer—Oh the sorry trade!

七十九

什么？他借出的只是破烂，
要他的造物用纯金偿还？
 我们何时曾向他借过债，
竟把这可悲的交易承担？

LXXX.

Oh Thou, who didst with pitfall and with gin
Beset the Road I was to wander in,
Thou wilt not with Predestin'd Evil round
Enmesh, and then impute my Fall to Sin!

八十

你啊，做了多少机关陷阱，
布满我流浪徘徊的路径。
别用命定的恶使我陷落，
再给我加上堕落的污名！

LXXXI.

Oh Thou, who Man of baser Earth didst make,
And ev'n with Paradise devise the Snake:
For all the Sin wherewith the Face of Man
Is blacken'd—Man's forgiveness give—and take!

八十一

你啊，造人是用卑贱之土，
给人的伊甸，也让蛇居住。
你宽恕罪人污浊的面容，
但自己也应该求人宽恕！

  神抟土造人，又造伊甸园让人居住，但也制造了引人堕落的魔鬼和引人犯错的种种诱惑。如此弄人，人又何辜？神才应该乞求宽恕。

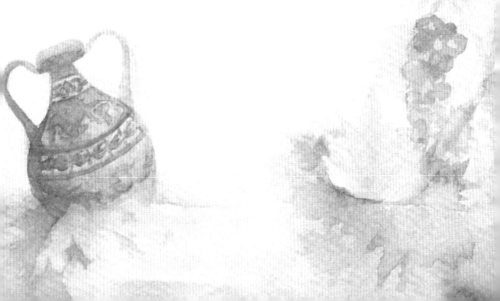

LXXXII.

As under cover of departing Day
Slunk hunger-stricken Ramazan away,
Once more within the Potter's house alone
I stood, surrounded by the Shapes of Clay.

八十二

黄昏的衣袍下白日将尽，
枯槁的斋月已从中遁形。
我又一次站在陶匠工坊，
身边围着些陶土的器皿。

　　伊斯兰历9月是斋月，教徒从日出至日落不得饮食。

　　从此节开始，有数节是陶匠和陶罐的比喻。陶匠喻神，造人犹如陶匠制作器皿。陶罐取自泥土。先前之人，已有多少化为泥土。诗人借陶罐之口，或感喟人生，或质疑宗教。

LXXXIII.

Shapes of all Sorts and Sizes, great and small,
That stood along the floor and by the wall;
And some loquacious Vessels were; and some
Listen'd perhaps, but never talk'd at all.

八十三

那大大小小的坛坛罐罐,
或立于地上,或倚在墙边。
有些喋喋不休,絮絮不止,
有些似在倾听,缄默无言。

LXXXIV.

Said one among them— "Surely not in vain
My substance of the common Earth was ta'en
And to this Figure molded, to be broke,
Or trampled back to shapeless Earth again."

八十四

其中一个说,"这绝非徒劳——
他从这泥土中选出质料,
塑成了器皿;将来又打碎,
或者踩踏成泥,形状全销。"

自相矛盾的说法。陶器有疑问,但又不愿承认,正如人对神的怀疑。神既造了人,何以又毁灭人?

LXXXV.

Then said a Second— "Ne'er a peevish Boy
Would break the Bowl from which he drank in joy;
And He that with his hand the Vessel made
Will surely not in after Wrath destroy."

八十五

第二个说,"再暴躁的孩童,
也不肯打烂心怡的水杯。
这器皿既是他亲手所制,
怎会因一时怒气而损毁?"

另一种观点的辩解:制造而后销毁,生人而又毁人,这肯定不是神的本意。

LXXXVI.

After a momentary silence spake
Some Vessel of a more ungainly Make;
"They sneer at me for leaning all awry:
What! did the Hand then of the Potter shake?"

八十六

一阵沉默之后,又有人言
——是一个奇形怪状的陶罐,
"别人都嘲笑我丑陋歪斜,
岂不该怪陶匠双手抖颤?"

　　人之不完美,人之缺陷,是否要归咎于造人的神?

LXXXVII.

Whereat some one of the loquacious Lot—
I think a Sufi pipkin—waxing hot—
"All this of Pot and Potter—Tell me then,
Who is the Potter, pray, and who the Pot?"

八十七

随后有个雄辩的小东西——
定是苏菲教徒——厉声喝止：
"陶匠与陶器原本是一体！
你说，谁是陶匠，谁是陶器？"

  伊斯兰教苏菲派的教义近于泛神论：神即宇宙，宇宙即神，神之灵充满宇宙。造物之神与造物本是一体。

LXXXVIII.

"Why," said another, "Some there are who tell
Of one who threatens he will toss to Hell
The luckless Pots he marr'd in making—Pish!
He's a Good Fellow, and 'twill all be well."

八十八

又一个道:"休要胡言乱语!
你们有人说,他边做陶器
边把做坏的器皿扔进地狱?
他至仁至慈,绝不会有事!"

　　威严暴怒的神,和至仁至慈的神,哪个才是真面目?也许只取决于人的猜测和喜好。懦弱者把希望寄托在神的善意。

LXXXIX.

"Well," murmured one, "Let whoso make or buy,
My Clay with long Oblivion is gone dry:
But fill me with the old familiar Juice,
Methinks I might recover by and by."

八十九

谁又低语:"管它谁造谁买,
闲放太久,干得都要裂开。
若给我灌满熟悉的酒浆,
兴许我还能再恢复过来。"

　　其他坛坛罐罐的神学争论,没什么意义。还不如灌满酒浆,一解身心之渴。

XC.

So while the Vessels one by one were speaking,
The little Moon look'd in that all were seeking:
And then they jogg'd each other, "Brother! Brother!
Now for the Porter's shoulders' knot a-creaking!"

九十

陶罐们且只顾你说我讲,
久盼的新月已窥进工坊。
它们推挤着叫到:"啊,兄弟,
马上就担在挑夫的肩膀!"

　　"久盼的新月":伊斯兰圣训中说斋月"见新月而封斋,见新月而开斋。"新月重现,斋月结束,次日开斋节是盛大的节日。

XCI.

Ah, with the Grape my fading life provide,
And wash the Body whence the Life has died,
And lay me, shrouded in the living Leaf,
By some not unfrequented Garden-side.

九十一

余生请为我准备好酒浆,
死后用美酒濯洗我皮囊。
以绿叶为尸布,将我掩埋
在偶有游人的花园之傍。

XCII.

That ev'n buried Ashes such a snare
Of Vintage shall fling up into the Air
As not a True-believer passing by
But shall be overtaken unaware.

九十二

从我的尸骨中生出葡萄,
盘结的藤蔓在空中缠绕。
一旦有真正的信徒路过,
无意间就被这罗网笼罩。

　　生前畅饮葡萄美酒,死后也要滋养葡萄。葡萄藤蔓像是罗网,哪怕是虔诚的信徒也会被它网住,被宗教之外的诗酒人生所吸引。

XCIII.

Indeed the Idols I have loved so long
Have done my credit in this World much wrong:
Have drown'd my Glory in a shallow Cup,
And sold my reputation for a Song.

九十三

我一直崇拜的那些伪神
早已经把我的德行毁损:
用浅浅杯盏溺杀我荣耀,
为一曲欢歌卖掉我名声。

  崇拜偶像即各种伪神,是一神教之大罪。这里的伪神,说的是纵酒欢歌的生活。后两句颇似柳永词:"忍把浮名,换了浅斟低唱。"

XCIV.

Indeed, indeed, Repentance oft before
I swore—but was I sober when I swore?
And then and then came Spring, and Rose-in-hand
My thread-bare Penitence apieces tore.

九十四

罢了，罢了，我已立誓忏悔！
只不知立誓时是醒是醉？
待到春风又起，玫瑰在握，
那一线悔意却又被扯碎。

　　似悔而实不悔。

XCV.

And much as Wine has play'd the Infidel,
And robb'd me of my Robe of Honor—Well,
I wonder often what the Vintners buy
One half so precious as the stuff they sell.

九十五

酒啊,像异教徒一般卑鄙,
总是剥走我体面的外衣。
我却常想,酒贩所购之物
怎堪比他所售之物珍奇?

  酒让人失态,但在诗人眼里,却是珍贵无比之物。

XCVI.

Yet Ah, that Spring should vanish with the Rose!
That Youth's sweet-scented manuscript should close!
The Nightingale that in the branches sang,
Ah whence, and whither flown again, who knows!

九十六

啊，阳春终将随玫瑰凋亡，
青春的书卷也快要合上，
夜莺虽还在枝头上欢歌，
谁知它何处来，又将何往？

　　重回时光易逝的咏叹。

XCVII.

Would but the Desert of the Fountain yield
One glimpse—if dimly, yet indeed, reveal'd,
To which the fainting Traveler might spring,
As springs the trampled herbage of the field!

九十七

只愿荒漠中那一眼清泉,
纵使再渺茫,也终能显现。
让衰竭的旅人朝它扑去,
像被踩踏的草重又复原。

XCVIII.

Would but some winged Angel ere too late
Arrest the yet unfolded Roll of Fate,
And make the stern Recorder otherwise
Enregister, or quite obliterate!

九十八

愿有翼的天使莫来太迟，
趁命运的卷轴未及收起，
令古板的书写员再删改，
或者干脆就抹除了重记。

卷轴书写完毕，就该卷起了。幻想能命运的卷轴在没有被书写完毕之前，可以删改它、重写它。

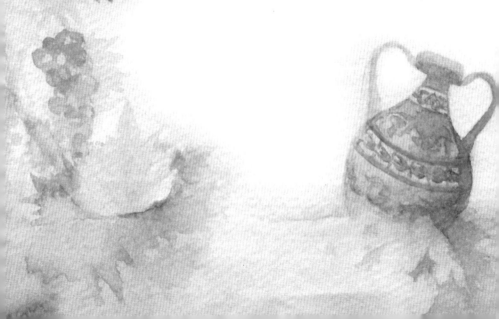

XCIX.

Ah Love! could you and I with Him conspire
To grasp this sorry Scheme of Things entire,
Would not we shatter it to bits—and then
Re-mold it nearer to the Heart's Desire!

九十九

爱人！若他肯与我们合计，
执掌这可悲的"万物之理"，
我们或可把它扯个粉碎，
按自己的心愿另行草拟！

　　"他"指上一节的"天使"，能否串通天使，修改神对万物、对命运的安排？显然也是幻想。

C.

Yon rising Moon that looks for us again—
How oft hereafter will she wax and wane;
How oft hereafter rising look for us
Through this same Garden—and for one in vain!

一百

明月初升,正把你我找寻,
今后它还有多少轮亏盈?
它还会升起,还会再寻觅,
花园依旧,那人已无踪影。

　　明月依旧,花园依旧,而斯人已不可寻。

CI.

And when like her, oh Saki, you shall pass
Among the Guests Star-scatter'd on the Grass,
And in your joyous errand reach the spot
Where I made One—turn down an empty Glass!

一百零一

酒童啊,你如明月般穿过
草坪上散落如星的酒客,
你欢跃而来,却只见空座——
扣上我的杯吧,我已陨殁。

　　酒童习惯性地来到这个常客的座位斟酒,但座位已空,斯人已逝。

رباعیات عمر خیام

برای اما، تنها خواننده در قلب من